MAKE $1,200 A MONTH WITH AIRBNB

BECOMING AN AIRBNB HOST

By

STEVE CHRYSTAL

Copyright © 2019

Introduction

My wife and I moved into a great 3-bedroom, 2 bath townhome, but quickly realized we had so much empty space just collecting dust. So, we decided to become Airbnb hosts! Neither one of us had ever hosted before, so we were total newbies. Although we had booked rooms through Airbnb before, hosting was a whole different ballgame.

There were many things to prepare for and plan, but none too difficult. The reward after putting in a little bit of effort is worth it.

So, in short, this book is for you! Pending, of course, you are interested in making money for renting your space. It's honestly very easy, and anyone can do it, trust me! While $1,200 a month may not seem like a ton of money to some, to others, it can make living much easier. Yes, there are some folks making huge incomes from Airbnb rentals, and they are likely telling the truth with their claims. The potential is there for sure, and depending on where you live and the demand, you could make way more than $1,200 a month!

Be sure to read until the end for a list of our favorite places to shop!

TABLE OF CONTENTS

Introduction

Table of Contents

Legal Notes

Chapter 1

How We Got Started

Chapter 2

Your Listing

Chapter 3

Pricing Your Listing

Chapter 4

Amenities

Chapter 5

Reviews Will Grow Your Income

Chapter 6

Guests

Chapter 7

How Long Until I'm Making $1,200?

Chapter 8

Tips on Cheap Decor

Legal Notes

We aren't telling you to jump right in without first consulting your local laws on Airbnb hosting. There has been a lot of laws put in place regarding Airbnb, so please be sure to read up and know them before you start. We are not held accountable for any issues you run into!

We obviously don't make any claims as to how much or how little you will make by hosting Airbnb. We share our own, unique story, so your earnings will be up to you.

Chapter 1

How We Got Started

In October 2017 my (soon to be) wife and I moved into our first place together. Yaaay! It was a lovely 3-bedroom, 2.5-bathroom townhome, tucked away at the end of a very quiet street, with only 4 homes in the row. About as quiet and relaxed as you could ask for in a townhome. It was in a wonderful location within the small, historic city in NC we lived in, and a couple other older homes in the area also ran Airbnb rentals, with great success.

Inside, the 2 level had the living room and kitchen downstairs, along with the half bath and garage. Upstairs, there were the 3 bedrooms, 2 sharing a hallway bathroom, and the master suite with a bathroom inside. The layout was convenient and smooth from a walking around perspective. The 2 bedrooms that would become rentals were located next to each other, so guests would have easy access and not disturb one another while coming and going.

Since the layout was welcoming, we had a good foundation for becoming hosts. If your home isn't laid out quite the same, it's ok. Almost every home can be made into a great space.

PREPARING THE SPACE

The home was only about 8 years old when we moved in, so everything was still very new and in great shape. The walls painted a neutral cream and the new carpet was a nice grey tone which made everything feel very clean. Clean is the keyword here, remember that!

Now, with the space being empty we had a good bit of prep to do. Add empty space on top of both of us not having a lot of stuff, and you get a real need for some décor shopping! This made my wife very happy, me, not so much. Just kidding, I also enjoy a good décor shopping day, as long as there is some beach themed action in there somewhere.

WHERE TO START

The first thing we decided to do was only rent one of the rooms to begin with. While we had two rooms sitting empty, we thought we would give one a shot since this was out first go at hosting. In our second room, we coincidentally found a semi long term roommate which funny enough came from an Airbnb contact. Long story for another time.

Since we had a room in desperate need of some beachy décor, we decided to tackle some décor shopping at one of our favorite (dangerous) places, Hobby Lobby! I'm sure you're a fan…

We started by picking out some nice curtains, which added to the clean look of the room. We found several other beach themed pieces that fit right in. We kind of put the cart before the horse when we sort of forget about a bed, woops! Luckily, a good friend had a mattress store nearby and was able to hook us up with a nice Queen bed set, which fit perfectly in the room. A good point is, don't try to stuff a super large bed in a room that won't support it. A King bed would have been way too much for the space and most people who are staying are totally fine with a Queen.

Now, by this point we had a clean, simple, themed room that was ready for guests! One other selling point I should touch on was the use of a theme of sorts. Most people love the beach, and even though we were about 5 hours from the nearest beach and in the mountains, a beach theme still worked great. Not saying you need to do the same but work any angles you can by setting yourself apart and appealing to more people. When folks are browsing listing in your area, chances are there are a lot to choose from and having something eye catching in the title and description might be what gets them to book with you instead of the next guy.

The space you are renting should feel welcoming. It's ok to not have a ton of things and stuff in the room. The majority of folks that stayed with us were traveling and having simple, effective, useful amenities was perfect. I know some of you might have a ton of stuff in your space, just make sure it's not overwhelming. Make sure the room is easily moved about and that there is space for the guest to put their things, like suitcase, bags, etc. Simple is good, don't overcomplicate it!

Now, if you have a luxury home, some of this might not apply to you. The luxury aspect of hosting is another book completely!

CHAPTER 2

Your Listing

Your listing is your representation of your space, it needs to be spot on. Everything from your title, description, and most importantly, photos needs to be super. If you have a good title but your photos look like crap, this is going to hurt your listing a lot. The pictures are the most important piece of the puzzle.

If you can take good shots, great. If you need help, get help! Don't let money fall through your fingers because of lack of effort!

Title, Description, & Photos

Let's start with the title of your listing. It should be a good indicator of what you're selling, because you are in fact selling here. Make it catchy, make it reflect your space, your home, and your décor. For our beach theme, we use Seaside Oasis as a title, and it worked great. It's catchy, and instantly perks people's interest.

Your description should be fairly in depth but straight forward. Don't add a ton of fluff here, describe everything as it is, describe your space and home, neighborhood, and what landmarks are around you. There are also a lot of SEO (Search Engine Optimization) that happens in your listing, but in this instance, we are focusing on getting started more so than tweaking your listing for search. Once you get the ball rolling, you'll still get views and bookings either way.

Your photos, ah yes, the car salesman of your listing. I will assume you have good idea on how you're going to layout and decorate your space, so let's get to the key points.

Stage your space. You want to make your space look and feel as if it were going to be featured in a magazine, because essentially, it will be. Make the bed, hang the curtains, arrange the décor, make sure it is spotless. Put the fancy bed sheets on the bed, layout the fancy towels, try to showcase all you will be offering your guests. We provided bottled water, towels, some themed soap and shampoo like you see in hotels. Make your guests feel comfortable before they even book your space. Make sure they see the spaces of your home that you will be sharing with them. If it's a room and shared bath, then make sure to show the bathroom space, perhaps the kitchen if you want to allow them to utilize that space as well.

You got this! Make it great, they will come!

Chapter 3

Pricing Your Listing

Pricing can be a tricky piece of the puzzle. Airbnb does a good job of giving you a consensus of about how much your listing is worth based on your location and demand in your area. Now, you may not always agree with what they suggest, but if you take into consideration what they base it on, the data they use, then it makes a little more sense.

Airbnb has a "smart pricing" tool which helps as well. Let's say you have a listing set at $50 a night, but there is a huge convention in town the next weekend, Airbnb's price tool will automatically increase the price along with the demand. This ends up putting more money in your pocket with no effort from you. You can also set minimums with this tool as well, meaning you'll always get whatever minimum price you set for your space. There are also options for discounts/coupons for your rentals. You can give discounts for longer stays and run promotions.

Valuating Your Space

If you are like us, we were renting rooms in our home. This means we were sharing our space with strangers. Yeah a little weird when you think about it, but look at it like short term roommates! You'll likely take this into consideration when you price your space, but don't let emotion get in the way of facts. If you overprice your space because you have to share with other people, then you'll likely get less bookings.

Airbnb has enough data now that their pricing suggestions are spot on in my opinion. We used the suggested pricing along with smart pricing, and never had any issues. The point is don't overprice your space. The one exception is if you have something that is unique or a space you cannot find anywhere else, like a treehouse or something wild like that. Obviously if you have an exotic space, you'll be charging a premium.

Price Competitively

Your space won't be the only space available. There will likely be lots of competition in your area, depending on where you live, of course. We had a little bit of competition because of the area which we were in, but nothing like somewhere such as New York City would have.

Research your competition. You should put in some work and research your area as if you are looking to stay there. Pretend your looking for a rental for the weekend in your city, see what others are doing, read their reviews, check out their listings. You'll learn a lot just by doing this, you can get a good feel for what is selling and what isn't. Check out some of their reviews left by people who've stayed with them. What are some things they like or dislike? Take notes, incorporate these findings in your own listing.

Chapter 4

Amenities

You're not a hotel, remember that. This could mean a couple things. You could either need to step up your amenities game or keep it under control. Let's look at the basics of what we offered in our rentals.

We tried to keep is relatively simple. What we learned was 95% of the people who stayed with us were just in need of a bed, shower, & safe place to relax. This doesn't mean we only offered them those things, but we also didn't go overboard and try to please everyone. We had WIFI, basic toiletries, water, extra blankets, phone chargers, a fan, and kept the temperature at a comfortable level. That's kind of it. Most people who stayed with us loved it. There were no complaints on not having enough. The point I want to make is, don't try to please everyone because it simply isn't going to happen. Give guests what they need to have a quiet, comfortable stay.

Going Out of Your Way

When we had guests coming, we were always there to meet and greet them. This was just one of my own rules, but I think it's a good thing to follow. You can get a good sense of people when you meet them in person, it's often very different than messaging via the Airbnb platform.

This would sometimes mean that we would have to go a little out of our way for guests. A few times, guest's travel plans got delayed and they weren't going to arrive until late, sometimes around midnight. Now, I am not saying you should stay up and wait, but if you do, it goes a long way in their eyes and that will reflect when they leave you a review.

In the past, when I was a guest at someone's home, they offered me a ride to the airport at 5am, which was beyond what you expect. Being kind goes a long way and will come back to you in the form of good reviews, just something to keep in mind when dealing with folks, even when their plans upset your plans.

Chapter 5

Reviews Will Grow Your Income

Reviews are maybe the biggest key in all of this. Getting a good review should be your goal from first step to the last. Your ultimate goal is reach Superhost status, which is Airbnb's badge of greatness. You have to maintain excellent reviews for this to happen, and once you reach that level, your listing will be shown to more people when they search. It's a pretty big deal.

Think about when you buy something from Amazon. If you see a product with 2 stars and a product with 5 stars, of course you're going to go with the 5 star product. It's been evaluated by others, given their stamp of approval, and thus make it stand out from the others. In reality, you have to be really bad as a host to get horrible reviews, and if that is the case, which I am sure it's not, maybe rethinking Airbnb is best!

Remember what you're getting paid for

Remember, all in all, this is easy money. It might require a little bit of effort to get going, but after it picks up steam, all you'll really need to do is clean the space, laundry, and freshen up. The rest is autopilot and once you're listing has good reviews, and you hit Superhost status, it will become easier. The money will flow and the work you must do will lessen, sounds great, doesn't it?

There are a lot of ways to make extra income at home, this might be one of the top picks. The good thing is if you get burned out or need a break, you can just pause your listing. You can also block out the schedule and only host when you want to, kind of like Uber, going online and offline whenever you want to.

CHAPTER 6

GUESTS

Not all guests are alike, and not to sound mean or classify anyone, you're going to get some strange ones, welcome to life. One thing to remember is your comfortability and safety are priority, without question. With Airbnb, you have the option of guests automatically booking your space or getting your approval first. I choose the latter. This simply gives me an opportunity to see if I am comfortable with the person before they just show up to my home. You'll likely get more bookings when folks can book automatically, but for me, having the extra control was worth whatever bookings I may have missed.

Sometimes you'll get newbies who don't have reviews and who haven't verified themselves with Airbnb, which is fine, we all start somewhere, but I want a chance to actually communicate with them before accepting their booking and revealing my address. Once you accept they can then see your location and address. While Airbnb does what they can to keep everyone safe, they certainly cannot control everything. If I get a request from someone with no reviews, no picture, no verification, the first thing I do is strike up a conversation with them to see if they are actually legit. I'll ask, politely, why they are coming into town, where they are from, and get a feel if they are, in fact, for real. This is just my method to help me feel better about who stays in my home. If you have a rental where you rent the entire home and you don't actually live there, then it might be a little different process for you, which is fine.

Be Respectful

Your guests will all be different. Unlike having a fulltime roommate who you eventually get to know and have a feel for how they are personality wise, Airbnb guests are different every time. You'll need to learn a little bit of flexibility, learn how to get a long with just about any type of person, and learn how to be neutral while making them comfortable at the same time.

CHAPTER 7

HOW LONG UNTIL I'M MAKING $1,200?

Great question! In all fairness, we were able to do all of this and reach Superhost status within 3 months! We started hosting the single room and then went on to rent out both spare rooms once our semi-permanent roommate left. When we first started, our earnings increased each month. These are our results, so we make no claim as to how much you'll make, but if you follow the advice from this book, you'll have a much better chance at hitting your income goals in no time.

CHAPTER 8

TIPS ON CHEAP DECOR

Some of our favorite shopping locations are listed below. For our beach themed rentals, we found a ton of good stuff at local stores as well as stores in actual beach towns. You can find a lot of cool stuff in coastal places, go figure!

1. Hobby Lobby – Great for cheap décor of any kind. They often have weekly or bi-weekly sales, sometimes with 50% off lots of items, so be sure to line up your shopping to take advantage of those!
2. Bed, Bath & Beyond – Great place for bedding, towels, etc. Can be a little on the expensive side, which we understand is not for everyone, so see number 3 for an alternative.
3. Wal-Mart – Yes, as much as I hate Wal-Mart, they have everything. Let's face it, they are a one stop shop for just about anything these days, don't fight it, you know you want to!

4. Big Lots – Not sure if these are all over the US, but Big Lots actually has a lot of good stuff for cheap. We've gotten things like towels, sheet sets, blankets, and even home décor and furniture there for pretty cheap prices.
5. Amazon.com – Of course Amazon is on this list. You most likely are very familiar with Amazon and have a bunch of empty Amazon boxes laying around your garage. Lots of good décor items on there for sure, and with Prime, they can be at your door pretty fast.

Steve Chrystal

Thanks for reading. I sincerely hope this book helped you in some way. If you have any questions, please don't hesitate to reach out. www.sea-sideoasis.com

CAN I ASK A FAVOR?

If you enjoyed this book, found it useful or otherwise then I'd really appreciate it if you would post a short review on Amazon. I do read all the reviews personally so that I can continually write what people are wanting.

Thanks for your support!

www.ingramcontent.com/pod-product-compliance
Lightning Source LLC
Chambersburg PA
CBHW030603220526
45463CB00007B/3165